W9-CKI-083

Presenting Yourself: Business Manners, Personality, and Etiquette

Earning $50,000–$100,000 with a High School Diploma or Less

Announcer

Car Mechanic

Chef

Cosmetologist

DJ

Dog Groomer

Energizing Energy Markets:
Clean Coal, Shale, Oil, Wind, and Solar

Farming, Ranching, and Agriculture

Masseur & Massage Therapist

Personal Assistant

Presenting Yourself: Business Manners,
Personality, and Etiquette

Referee

The Arts: Dance, Music, Theater, and Fine Art

Truck Driver

Earning $50,000–$100,000
with a High School Diploma or Less

Presenting Yourself: Business Manners, Personality, and Etiquette

Christie Marlowe

Mason Crest

Mason Crest
450 Parkway Drive, Suite D
Broomall, PA 19008
www.masoncrest.com

Printed in the United States of America.

First printing
9 8 7 6 5 4 3 2 1

Series ISBN: 978-1-4222-2886-9
ISBN: 978-1-4222-2898-2
ebook ISBN: 978-1-4222-8934-1

The Library of Congress has cataloged the
        hardcopy format(s) as follows:

            Library of Congress Cataloging-in-Publication Data

Marlowe, Christie.
  Presenting yourself : business manners, personality, and etiquette / Christie Marlowe.
      pages cm. − (Earning $50,000-$100,000 with a high school diploma or less)
  Includes bibliographical references and index.
  Audience: Grade 7 to 8.
  ISBN 978-1-4222-2898-2 (hardcover) − ISBN 978-1-4222-2886-9 (series) − ISBN 978-1-4222-8934-1 (ebook)
  1. Business etiquette–Juvenile literature. 2. Vocational guidance–Juvenile literature. I. Title.
  HF5389.M374 2014
  395.5'2–dc23
                            2013015570

Produced by Vestal Creative Services.
www.vestalcreative.com

Contents

CHAPTER 1
Careers Without College

M any careers and professional fields are available for anyone who does not want to spend time and money on a college education. Young people, told that a college diploma is the *only* safe bet when it comes to finding a well-paying and stable career, often overlook these careers.

Above all else, what a young person should learn from the other books in this series is that a college education is *one* option—an option that should certainly be considered—but not the *only* option for someone looking for success and a fulfilling career.

College can be a great time for learning from both professors and other people your own age.

PRESENTING YOURSELF

No College Education Required

A college education can be a wonderful thing. Education, no matter where and how you get it, is a valuable tool in life—and college is one of the most exciting and intellectually stimulating places to get an education. There are some careers where four years of college—or many more than that—are absolutely required for even an **entry-level** position. You're never going to become a doctor or a lawyer without spending lots of time in college and university classrooms!

College is also often the first time that many young people leave home and live without the safety and security of their parents. Most colleges also offer courses and programs in areas that might not seem directly applicable to a work situation but are important for building a young person's understanding of people, cultures, arts, and sciences, which may not be available to them otherwise. You never know what seemingly unrelated piece of knowledge could trigger your imagination and get you started on the road to success. Steve Jobs, for example, college dropout and founder of Apple Inc., attributed the inspiration for his innovative designs to a calligraphy course he took when he was a young man.

Similarly, college can be the time where young people learn important "soft-skills," such as cooperation and compromise. Having a roommate, learning to interact with your peers on campus, and

Looking at the Words

A beginning job in a career, requiring minimal skills, knowledge, and experience, is called an **entry-level** position.

Getting a college diploma is a great achivement, but there are other routes you could take to a successful future.

experiencing **mentoring** relationships with professors are all life-shaping opportunities.

That being said, college is not the only place where someone can broaden her horizons or learn how to live without mom and dad. Some people, like John Tamny, political and economic writer for *Forbes Magazine*, have even questioned the idea that a college education is necessary to learn the skills required for even those careers that require a college diploma. He writes, "[Barack] Obama is President of the United States and [Jane] Shaw [is] President of a prestigious think tank, but could either with a straight face point to anything learned in college that has any **relevance** to their present work?"

As Tamny suggests, the skills learned in college do not necessarily translate to success once a college graduate has begun a career. Most of these skills, according to Tamny, are learned on the job. Despite this, the employers of certain careers continue to require a college diploma before they will even consider your application. This is because, as Tamny writes, "A college diploma is simply a **credential** that at best says you're smart and **ambitious**." Tamny is writing in reaction to politicians who insist on the need to see more young people in America graduating from college.

Students at vocational schools often receive practical, on-the-job training.

According to the Bureau of Labor Statistics, nearly 70 percent of high school graduates in 2011 went on to attend college. Unfortunately, though certain career paths require a college education, a college education isn't necessarily a safe bet when it comes to finding a successful career. According to CNN, the average student, in 2012, graduated college nearly $27,000 in debt, a debt that takes an average of ten years to pay off. CNN also reported that half of all college graduates were either unable find a job or they found a job that didn't even require a college degree!

The Bureau of Labor Statistics also reports that fifteen of the thirty fastest growing jobs in America do not require a four-year college education. Quickly growing jobs offer more opportunities for employment, less competition for the available positions, fewer lay-offs, and, usually, faster and more substantial wage increases than other careers.

Getting one of these jobs, though, doesn't mean you can simply graduate from high school and show up. Almost all careers require some sort of training after high school. A good alternative to a college degree, however, is to attend a training program or "vocational" school, a school that trains you for a specific career but is shorter and much cheaper than a traditional four-year college. Vocational school programs can last from six months to two years. They can also be completed part time, so that students can work other jobs and support themselves while they acquire new skills.

Some well-paying careers that do not require a college education—truck drivers and dog groomers, for example, both of which are adding more than 20 percent more jobs between 2010 and 2020—offer nearly free or on-the-job training. Similar to on-the-job training are **apprenticeships**, like those offered to electricians, another career expected to add more than 20 percent more jobs before 2020. Apprentices usually have very little prior experience, but they are hired by a company in order to be taught while they work. Apprenticeships can be longer than a vocational school, typically about four years, and sometimes involve classes at local community colleges. Careers like truck driving, dog grooming, and being an electrician offer the possibility of making over $50,000 a year—and there are many other well-paying and fulfilling careers that can be acquired through vocational schools, apprenticeships, or on-the-job training as well.

Knowing what careers are the fastest growing and the highest paying, understanding how you can become prepared for these careers and how much time and money this training costs, and (perhaps most important) becoming aware of what kind of work you would like to do and how hard you are willing to work to become prepared—these are the factors to consider carefully before deciding whether or not to go to college.

Preparing Yourself for the Job Hunt

Preparing yourself for the job hunt means many things. In short, looking for a career can be broken down into five categories.

- Research: finding out information about fields of work where you might want to work, companies you might like to work for, salaries that you could make, and the careers that are most available to you based on your experiences and location.
- Contacts: people who can help you learn and research jobs. They are those people who can eventually be useful for recommending you to **potential** employers. The people whom you know are known as your "network," and meeting new people who might be able to help you find a career is known as "networking."
- Skills and training: not only the **practical** skills that you will use on a job, like those learned in a vocational school or college, but also career counseling and learning how to be interviewed with confidence by a potential employer.
- Résumé: a summary of your experiences and skills that are relevant to the position or career where you are looking to apply.

Preparing a résumé involves not only learning what it should look like and what to include on it but also includes knowing where to post it so that potential employers with open positions will be able to see it.

- Searching for vacancies: knowing where potential employers post advertisements for open positions and being able to find where to look for the careers that would be most suited to you and your experiences.

Reading about and researching these categories (like you are doing now!) is an important step and a great way to prepare yourself for what can be the difficult process of seeking a career. If you have prepared yourself well, not much will surprise you once you begin to look for a career.

Luckily, most of us already have access to a tool that can be very important when it comes to preparing yourself and eventually hunting for a career: a computer. The Internet can be a powerful tool for a new applicant entering the job hunt. Websites such as the Bureau of Labor Statistics (bls.gov) and PayScale (payscale.com) can be great resources for learning about careers and expected salaries. Many websites offer suggestions or **templates** for building an attractive and appealing résumé. Others—like Indeed (indeed.com), Monster (monster.com), and Craigslist (craigslist.org)—are great places to post your résumé and find job

Looking at the Words

Potential means having the capacity to become or develop into something in the future.

If something is **practical**, it is useful or related to manual tasks.

Templates are models to copy.

vacancies. You'll still need to learn social skills and networking, but the Internet can help you meet new people, get interviews, and find career counseling centers (places where you can improve your résumé or take practice interviews). Learning all the possibilities that the Internet has to offer can be an important first step on the road to finding a career.

Presenting Yourself

No matter how you hunt for jobs, whether on the Internet or in your local newspaper's "want ads," you will be, in all instances, expected to treat any contacts or potential employers with a certain amount of respect. In fact, being respectful to all people (since you never know who can or will be a useful contact) can greatly improve your chances of getting a job. Your manners, personality, and appearance will show these people that you have respect for them and will allow these people to see you in your best possible light. Contacts will be more willing to recommend you to any employers they might know—and employers will be more likely to see the reasons to hire you before they notice any reasons they might not want to hire you. Being able to show others respect through your manners, appearance, and personality is known as "presenting yourself." It can be, above all else, the most important skill for finding a career.

All employers, whether they require applicants to have a college degree or not, expect new employees to be hard working and respectful. Therefore, whether you are applying to be a sales clerk at a local fast-food chain or the CEO of a Fortune 500 company, it is your responsibility, as an applicant, to show a potential employer not only that you are going to work hard for him but also that you take yourself and the position that you are applying for seriously. This is another way to present yourself well.

Presenting yourself in your best possible light may not come naturally. It may mean practicing new skills. It could require taking a look

at yourself and your habits—your **etiquette**, personal hygiene, personality, and appearance—in order to make them look as good as possible! This doesn't mean that you have to put on a big act or fake who you really are. But you want your appearance to represent you and your **work ethic**.

When employers are interviewing for a job opening,

they generally have a few traits they are looking for in an employee. For example, a well-organized individual is often times able to work faster and is able to work better in team situations. Having organization means always knowing where to look for something and being able to easily communicate to others where they can look for something that they might need. It means employees don't waste time figuring out where things are and what they should be doing. Organization is an important quality in most work situations. But if a potential employee walks into an interview late or with a messy briefcase, that tells an interviewer the person was able to organize neither his time nor his personal belongings. You may think it's no big deal to be a few minutes late for an interview—but it could be the detail that makes the employer decide not to hire you.

This may not seem fair to you. Maybe you just had a bad day. Maybe something came up that was out of your control, something that got you off to a bad start that morning and had you running late. But an interviewer doesn't know all that. She has a half hour or so to decide what she thinks about you. She probably has several other applicants to compare you to as well. In a situation like that, details matter!

Careers Without College   17

Good etiquette means a lot more than how you hold your tea-cup! It has far more to do with qualities like respect and courtesy.

Nancy R. Mitchell, the founder of The Etiquette Advocate, a firm that provides etiquette training and consulting to large organizations, writes, "Your attitude and behavior toward others are as important as your résumé, experience, training and technical abili-

ties." No matter how much experience or how many degrees you have, one thing that can immediately disqualify you for a career is if you present yourself poorly. While factors like the appearance of your résumé are important, businesses, according to Mitchell, "are looking for the human qualities that make the difference in business relationships: courtesy, respect, trust and **reliability**. Manners and respect are the underlying foundation of good relationships, and good relationships translate to business success."

Being able to present yourself well shows that you, as an employee, will represent your employer to the best of your ability. Believe it or not, when it comes to landing your dream job, presenting yourself well could be even more important than whether you decide to go to college!

CHAPTER 2

Etiquette, Manners, and Communication

E tiquette and manners are very similar concepts and practices. Both refer to guidelines for behavior deemed acceptable by a specific group of people or society. They are like laws in that they guide us toward what is considered correct or appropriate behaviors and practices—but unlike laws, no individual or government has been put in charge of enforcing these guidelines. It is up to you, and no one else, to display good manners and proper etiquette!

Etiquette in Other Times and Other Parts of the World

Proper etiquette has very few hard-and-fast rules. If we were able to take a ride in a time machine, we would be able to see many different examples of etiquette, depending on what time period we were traveling through. For example, during the Middle Ages, it was good etiquette to give a male guest a bath—but in today's world, a guest would be pretty surprised if he arrived to find a bubble bath waiting for him!

Proper etiquette also varies geographically. In America, for example, it is considered polite to make eye contact with someone when she is speaking to you—but in other countries, it is considered rude to stare someone in the eye when he is talking to you. In America, it is common to whistle when applauding at a concert—but in other parts of the world, whistling is considered rude, more akin to booing.

If you travel outside your home country, make sure you are aware of what is considered proper etiquette where you are traveling!

Good Manners, Proper Etiquette

Etiquette and manners differ in terms of when and why they are used. Manners are general guidelines for behavior that apply to all situations. Examples of good manners include actions that are always appropri-

ate, such as saying "please" and "thank you," and general rules such as always treating the elderly with respect. Etiquette, on the other hand, refers to guidelines that are specific to a given situation, such as knowing which fork to use during the second course of a dinner or making sure that you begin a formal e-mail with a salutation such as "Dear Ms. Smith." A person might possibly have very good manners while knowing very little about etiquette.

In the business world, understanding this difference between etiquette and manners can be important. Good manners are practiced across all cultures, while etiquette tends to vary between cultures. For example, saying thank you, listening with respect when someone is talking, and answering when you are spoken to are behaviors that are considered good manners pretty much around the world. On the other hand, a firm and confident handshake is considered good etiquette when initially meeting someone in America—but in China, this is not the case. Chinese business people often greet a person by offering a business card that should, according to Chinese etiquette, be graciously accepted and read immediately.

Both manner and etiquette demonstrate to employers that you are respectful, considerate, and mature. These are all traits that are valued in any job.

- **Respect** means recognizing other people's value as human beings regardless of their background, race, class, age, gender, or sexuality. It means refusing to do certain things, like laughing at **racist** or **sexist** jokes. You

Your look may express who you are—but showing respect and maturity in most work settings means you keep this look for weekends only.

won't base your opinion of others on unfair and **biased** assumptions. Respect for others also means you're on time (recognizing that others' time is as important as yours). It means you dress appropriately for the work setting, and you are **attentive** to others.

Looking at the Words

Biased means having unfair favor for or against.

To be **attentive** is to notice others and treat them well.

Recruiters are people who search for job candidates for a company.

- **Consideration** is the act of behaving thoughtfully, aware of others' feelings. It means understanding that your actions have an effect on others, and it means you are willing to accommodate others' needs. A considerate person offers help where it is needed and appreciates help when it is offered.
- **Maturity** means being able to adjust your behavior for different settings. You don't talk too loudly and distract others in a quiet room where everyone is working; you don't interrupt people when they are talking. You don't laugh or make jokes during a serious moment, and you don't use crude words or tell off-color jokes in the workplace. You pick up on social cues as to what is expected of you; you don't overreact to frustration or get your feelings hurt easily.

These are the foundations for good manners and proper etiquette—and good manners and proper etiquette can be the features that set you apart from a candidate with similar skills and education. According to company **recruiters** and hiring managers nationwide, proper etiquette among young people entering the job market is poor, at best. So if you

Keeping close track of time is one way to show respect and maturity in the work world.

work hard to be sure that you have these qualities, you will already have an edge when it comes to competing in the job market. You'll stand out compared to other job seekers.

Some general etiquette guidelines for employment situations include:

- **Research each company and position that you apply for.** At the very least, look up the company online and, if possible, understand where the company is headed and what kind of services it provides.
- **Examine your writing.** Every time you send out any sort of communication (whether through the mail or e-mail), make sure that it is free of spelling or grammatical errors. If possible, have someone else look over your letters and résumé to get a fresh pair of eyes.
- **Dress appropriately.** Proper dress etiquette for employment situations includes clean and wrinkle-free clothes. For most interviews, you will want to wear formal business attire. Jewelry and hair-dos should be professional and **conservative**, and tattoos should be hidden.
- **Be on time.** Timeliness is important because it proves that you are considerate. If you show up to an interview late, you have just wasted some of the interviewer's time. You have already cost the company money before even stepping in the door!
- **Have an appropriate attitude.** Be enthusiastic about the position that you are applying for or the work that you are doing. This includes being friendly to others and wearing a confident smile. A lack of enthusiasm in an employment situation is probably a sign that you are working in the wrong field!

You may not mean to be rude, but if you text during an interview, you communicate that you don't consider the interview to be as important to you as talking to your friends.

It is often said that manners and etiquette are the arts of making others feel comfortable—so while etiquette involves some very specific rules, as long as you make an honest attempt at making others feel comfortable, you will, at the very least, be on the right track!

Respectful Communication

You may have noticed that the general employment etiquette rules listed above deal in some way with communication. Communication, in the broadest sense of the word, is the activity of sharing or conveying information between two or more people.

Communication happens many ways—speech, visual signs (appearance, dress, and body language), writing, and behavior—and always involves at least three things: a sender, a message, and a recipient. It is important to remember these three parts because when you are communicating, especially in the case of an employment situation, you need to be aware of the fact that a message may not be understood by the receiver in the way you intended.

In America, for example, shaking your head up and down means "yes" and shaking it side to side means "no." In parts of the Middle East, it is the other way around. An American in the Middle East might be sending a message that to her means "yes," while a Middle Easterner might receive the meaning as "no." Although the people you interact with in most job situations will probably understand what you mean if you shake or nod your head, they may misunderstand other messages you are sending. For example, many young people text while they are talking with their friends. They mean no disrespect to their friends, and their friends aren't offended (especially, since they're probably texting too). But if you text during a job interview, your interviewer is likely to receive the message that you consider your text conversation more

Being able to get along with others is vital to almost any work you do.

important than the interview—even if that wasn't at all the message you meant to send.

Any communication with a potential employer requires honest, clear, and considerate communication. A job interview is not the place to express your inmost feelings by wearing a bizarre outfit or bursting into song! Communication that is considerate of the receiver is always aware of all of the messages you're sending, even when you may not have intended to send a message at all. For example, you may intend the tattoo of a tree on your arm to communicate your love of nature—but it may communicate to a job interviewer a very different message about the sort of person you are. Body language is another example of communication that will take place in a job interview. If you slouch in your seat, you will indicate a lack of respect to the interviewer, while if you sit up straight, you communicate both respect and maturity.

Respectful communication involves both the content of your message and the way in which it is delivered. The content of your résumé, for example, refers to what experiences you include on it. How this information is conveyed, on the other hand, refers to your résumé's appearance—what font you use, how large your margins are, the kind of paper you used. The experiences and credentials listed on your résumé might be amazingly impressive—but if your résumé is difficult to read or unprofessional looking, potential employers are unlikely to read far enough to be impressed by the credentials you've listed.

Respectful communication conveys information thoughtfully, honestly, and considerately. Respectful communication is at the core of building positive and healthy relationships. You might think that the ability to form relationships has very little to do with getting a job—but the fact is, relationships are at the core of both finding a job and being successful once you have started work.

Resume

John Q. Doe
1234 Suburban Way
Averageville, NA 02345
Phone: 789-555-9876
E-mail: johnd@fakeemail.com

Objective: Job ID 99999

QUALIFICATIONS

- Great people skills
- 18 years of experience in the field
- Management potential
- Highly organized and efficient
- Team player
- Experience dealing with client needs and resolving issues
- Proficient in Computer Systems

WORK EXPERIENCE & ACHIEVEMENTS

Computer Systems Analyst   2005 to 2010
Big International Corporation

Computer programmer   1992 to 2005
Technology Firm

Customer Service Representative   1985 to 1992
Car Rental Agency

EDUCATION

MBA 1988
University of My State

CHAPTER 3

Writing a Résumé

A résumé is a summary of the experiences and skills relevant to the field of work that you are hoping to enter. It includes an overview of your accomplishments, shows a potential employer that you are **qualified** for the work you want to do, and (ideally) demonstrates why you, above all others considered for the job,

Contact Information
phone
site
email

resume

NAME SURNAME

professional title

■ **objective**

■ **qualification**

■ **professional experience**

■ **education**

Here are the elements that every résumé should include. You can organize them a bit differently, but make sure the layout is clean, clear, and professional.

would be best suited for the particular position that you are applying for.

When it comes to communication, your résumé is often the first thing that you communicate to a pote tial employer. Therefore, learning how to write a clear, **effective** résumé is perhaps one of the most important steps toward finding a career.

What to Include, What Not to Include

Even as a young person, you already have had many experiences, many of which may seem extremely important to you. What may seem like an important experience to you, however, may not be considered important by a potential employer! Choosing wisely which of these experiences to include on a résumé informs an employer of only those reasons that she should hire you. It communicates to an employer that you understand all the skills you will need to be successful if you're offered the position. Remaining considerate of a potential employer also means you understand that she only wants to hear about those experiences of yours that make you a good match for the position. (She's really not interested in hearing about how good you are at computer games or your amazing scuba-diving vacation—unless either of those applies in some way to the job opening.)

Some information should always be included on a résumé, such as your contact information (including your name, address, e-mail address, and phone numbers) and a few references—people who will speak well of

either your character, skills, or work ethic on your behalf. When it comes to your experiences, all potential employees want to see three kinds of experience listed: your work history, your education, and your relevant skills (including knowledge of software, machines, and/or tools).

Your résumé is a record of your life's accomplishments, so while you want to keep it relevant to the position that you are applying for, make sure that you allow yourself to brag a little. While humility is an admirable trait, it is a very difficult thing to communicate through a résumé. Your potential employer will assume you listed the most admirable experiences of your life on a résumé, so do not hold back. When you list your work history, for example, list in detail your responsibilities and accomplishments related to your work, especially any accomplishments that exhibit skills relevant to the company and position that you are applying for. Present yourself in the best possible light. On the other hand, don't exaggerate your past experiences; for instance, if you were in charge of taking out the trash for an office, don't say you were the office manager!

You may also want to include your hobbies and volunteer activities, if they demonstrate something about you that makes you more qualified for a job. A young person who has just entered the job market, for example, would want to include any extracurricular activities that she may have participated in during her time in high school (especially those in which she took a leadership role), any volunteer work she has done, and any internships that she has completed. If you're applying for your first job working in a daycare facility, and you have no formal experience but you've been taking care of your little brother and sister every day after school for their entire lives, make sure your résumé communicates that!

Someone who is older and has more work experience, however, would probably want to stay away from mentioning high school experiences on his résumé, because this communicates to a potential employer that he hasn't done much since high school. Your most recent experiences are those that you want to spend the most time describing.

The important rule to remember when considering what to include on a résumé is that an employer is only interested in those experiences that demonstrate your skills. For example, being the captain of a high school sports team shows that you have exhibited leadership skills and an ability to direct others, skills that are highly valued by most employers.

You will probably apply to multiple companies and, sometimes, even entirely different fields at the same time, so you may want to consider targeting your résumé. This means you remove all **irrelevant** skills and experiences from the list. When applying for a job as an electrician, for example, your experience babysitting may be completely irrelevant for the work you will be doing. Including irrelevant skills and experiences may communicate to a potential employer that you do not fully understand the skills that are required to be successful in a particular position. It can also tell the employer that you are sending your résumé to other companies as well. As an applicant, you always want a potential employer to think you are completely focused on him and his company.

Writing a Cover Letter

A cover letter is a document sent with a résumé that provides additional information on your skills and experience. Besides targeting your résumé, a cover letter is one of the best ways to prove to a potential employer why you are a good fit for her company.

A cover letter will be effective if it explains both the reasons for your interest in the company (what you think the strong points of the

company are, for example) and how your strengths, skills, and past experiences will **complement** and improve the company. Exhibiting this requires tact, as you want to show that your skills will improve the company while also highlighting what you think the company is already doing well. You don't want to say, "I notice you have a really ugly website, and I could help you improve it with my graphic design skills"! Remaining positive on both sides will make employers think about what you can do for them without making them defensive. Criticizing your potential employer in any way will also come across as disrespectful. At the very least, a cover letter should express a high level of interest and knowledge about the position.

If you are sending your résumé through the mail, the cover letter will be a separate sheet of paper that is put in the envelope on top of the résumé. If you're sending your résumé via e-mail, the résumé will likely be an attachment, while the cover letter is in the body of the e-mail. The cover letter is one more opportunity for you to communicate respect and maturity. Do not miss this chance to prove to a potential employer that you are well suited for the position.

Your Résumé's Appearance

You want your résumé to stand out from others—but that is no reason to try out some of the fancy new fonts you just downloaded. What may appear attractive to you might look ugly, flashy, or just plain silly to an employer.

Play it safe—but at the same time, remember that employers are busy people who will spend, on average, only thirty seconds looking at a ré-

sumé. You want to quickly direct the employer's eye to the most important information. Therefore, your résumé needs to be, if possible, no more than a page long, and it should be clear and easy to read.

Looking at the Words

To **complement** means to enhance or improve.

Remember: having good manners and proper etiquette means showing consideration for what a potential employer expects from you. Your résumé is not the place to demonstrate your originality by listing your credentials in poem form or by scribbling cute little doodles in the margins.

Some tips on formatting a résumé include:

- Your résumé's format should be consistent. Don't switch fonts midline, for example.
- One-inch margins are standard for all pages.
- Font size should be between 10 and 12. Your name (placed at the top of your résumé) should be slightly larger.
- Easy to read fonts include: Times New Roman, Arial, Century, MS Sans Serif, Book Antiqua, Century Gothic, and Calibri.
- An uncluttered document is visually pleasing so do not make your résumé too crowded. You want lots of empty space on that page, so do not over-describe any experiences.
- Make sure to highlight any experiences you want your employer to see by **boldfacing** or *italicizing* them. But remember: keep your layout consistent. This means you may want to make all the main headings bold and italicize all your past titles, or something similar.
- If printing and mailing your résumé, do not use cheap paper (it

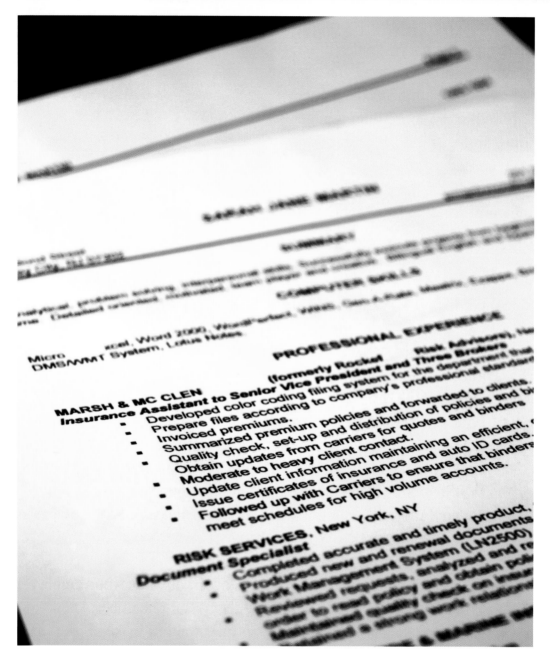

For some jobs, a very plain and businesslike résumé like this one may be the best choice.

should be at least 25 percent cotton) and only print on white, off-white, or light-gray paper. Do not use colored paper.

- Proofread your résumé carefully. Have someone else proofread it too. Spelling or grammatical mistakes communicate to an employer that you may be careless, a trait that no employer values!

There are three kinds of résumés: chronological, functional, and a combination of the two. The differences between them only have to do with what order you are listing your experiences.

"Chronological" means that events are arranged in the order of the time that they occurred. A chronological résumé starts by listing your work history, with the most recent position listed first, and then your education and skills after this. Chronological résumés can be difficult to target. You do not want to leave out any work experiences, however work experiences that are not relevant to the position that you are applying for should not be explained or explained only briefly.

A functional résumé is rarely used and highlights only relevant skills, education, and past work experience. Job seekers who are changing careers or did not work for a significant amount of time typically use a functional résumé. A gap in your work history will be very apparent on a chronological résumé, therefore a functional résumé can be used to make this gap less apparent and still demonstrate the relevant skills.

A combination of the two might be your best bet, especially for a young person, because a combination résumé is the easiest to target. A combination résumé lists your skills, education, and relevant experiences first and then your work history after, in chronological order.

If you have any more questions about your résumé, remember that the Internet is one of your best tools. There are many easy-to-use and attractive templates for your résumé on the Internet and plenty of tips on

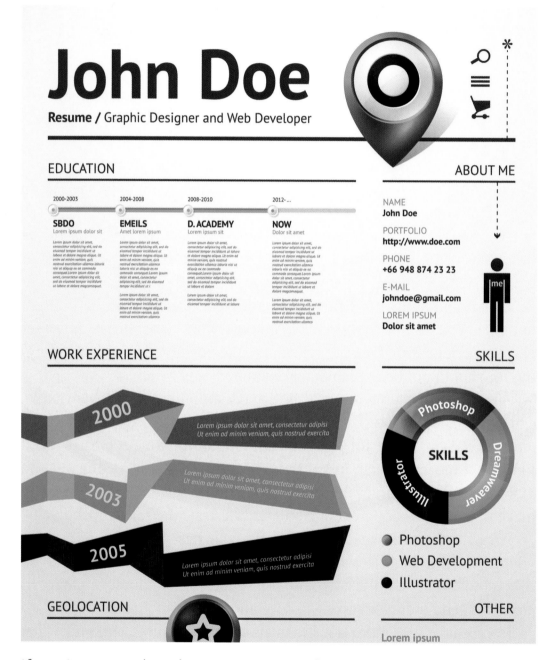

If you're a graphic designer, you might want to create an unsual résumé that showcases your skills.

formatting an attractive résumé. Make sure to research and learn all that you can in order to present yourself as confidently as you can!

Résumés for Creative Careers

The only situation where you will want to stray from a professional, conservative résumé is when you are applying for an art or design position, especially if the company to which you are applying is very cutting edge. In that case, you want your résumé to showcase your own design skills and creativity—and you want it to stand out from all the other résumés being submitted. You might want to also include some examples of your work on a CD or a link to your portfolio online. Your résumé still needs to be clear and readable—it shouldn't be so creative that the busy employer would have to spend more than 30 seconds deciphering it—but expressing yourself through your résumé for a creative job can be a good way to demonstrate what you have to offer the employer.

CHAPTER 4

Interview Etiquette

For entry-level positions at chain stores you may be able to land a job just by filling out an application—but things are not so simple when it comes to finding a career. A career is more than just a job; it is the course of work you will be taking up for a long period of time, sometimes your entire life. A potential employer is very aware of this, which makes his hiring choices all the more important. This is going to be a long-term relationship! Imagine if you were about to invite someone into your family.

During a job interview, your clothes, your body language, your expression, and your words should all communicate your self-confidence, maturity, and respect.

You would want to know more about her than just what a single piece of paper could tell you.

An interview is a meeting with someone at a company who will be in control of whether or not you get hired. It is where you will discuss, face-to-face, your qualifications for a job. When applying for a career, an effective résumé will be able to get you an interview—and an interview is the place where your etiquette, manners, and personality will be most important!

First Impressions

An employer spends only about thirty seconds looking at a résumé, and it takes a similar amount of time (between thirty seconds and four minutes) for an employer to begin to form an opinion of a potential employee. The first few minutes of an interview is known as a first impression, and you don't want to miss this chance to begin to form the image of yourself that you want to leave in the mind of your interviewer.

If an employer wants to interview you, she'll probably either give you a telephone call or send you an e-mail. If a potential employer calls, make sure to use your phone etiquette. Say "Hello, this is [your name] speaking," when you answer (don't say, "Yo!"), and speak slowly and clearly. If you answer by e-mail, make sure you proofread your writing, begin the e-mail with a **salutation**, and make sure to sign the e-mail with your full name.

If you are unavailable during the time when a potential employer asks you to come in for an interview, inform him of this and ask if there are any other times

Looking at the Words

A **salutation** is a greeting.

Be careful that your expression and posture aren't saying something you don't mean to communicate. You want your interviewer to feel that you're excited about the job—not sad, bored, or lacking in confidence

that are convenient for him. Attempt to be as accommodating as possible to any potential employers; being accommodating means that you are willing to fit in with someone else's wishes in a helpful way. Since you are applying to help a company, being accommodating communicates that you will be helpful once you have been hired. So be careful about deciding to say you're unavailable. If you have a doctor's appointment, that's one thing—but if you planned to hang out with a friend, you should probably ask your friend to reschedule rather than the potential employer.

When entering an interview, be enthusiastic and have energy. Smiling is an important sign of your personality. Would you want to invite someone into your family who wasn't happy to be part of it? Shake hands with each person who will be interviewing you and introduce yourself with your first and last name.

Make sure to be aware of your posture. Don't slump or hunch over. Don't sprawl in the chair or put your feet up. An open, respectful posture means keeping your shoulders square with the person that you are speaking to. This communicates an openness and willingness to listen.

Do not sit down unless you are asked to sit. If you are not asked to sit immediately, politely ask where your interviewer would like you to be seated. When sitting, plant your feet firmly on the floor, keep a straight back, and do not cross your arms or legs. If you are asked if you would like a drink, politely decline (you don't want to end up spilling it all over yourself or your interviewer!), and if you have brought anything with you, place it on the floor beside your seat. Once sitting, you hands should be placed on your thighs. Do not fidget in your chair and try not to use too many hand gestures. When people are nervous, they often move their hands far too much. Remember, presenting yourself is about making yourself look as natural as possible, so try not to appear nervous.

Business clothes will help people take you seriously, even if you're young.

PRESENTING YOURSELF

Your Appearance

An important part of a first impression has to do with what you have worn to the interview. People show respect for an organization, individual, or event by dressing up. Dressing appropriately communicates to an employer that she matters and that you respect her and her business.

It is critical to be clean from your head to your toes. Any creative piercings, hair-dos, and tattoos should be left at home or concealed. If you wear glasses, make sure that the lenses are clean. Do not wear cologne or perfume, and check your face, teeth, and clothes before you enter the room. Fresh breath is a must, but do not chew on gum or suck on any mints. Remember that your appearance sends messages whether you want it to or not, so make sure to dress as well as you can!

Formal business attire is considered proper etiquette for any interview. Formal business attire for men includes: a suit that is either gray, navy, or charcoal; a clean, pressed white shirt; a conservative tie (tie-a-tie.net can show you how to tie it properly!); dark, over-the-calf socks that match your suit (no white athletic socks with your nice suit!); a black leather belt; and black leather shoes that are polished. Formal business attire for women includes: a dark suit (if you are wearing a suit skirt, the skirt should be knee length); a light-colored blouse; polished, professional shoes (no large heels or open-toe shoes); and, if you are wearing a suit skirt, pantyhose that are light in color or match your skin tone.

There is an old adage, "Dress for the career that you want to have." A well-dressed person will be that much more confident and will be showing the respect that he has for the situation he is in. You are on a stage the

Everyone feels nervous sometimes at a job interview. Just be yourself. Remind yourself that whether you get the job or not, you can learn something from the experience.

moment you walk into the building where the interview will take place, so make sure that your costume is flawless!

Personality

No one should ever underestimate the power of people skills in an interview. If an interviewer likes you, he will hope you will do well. He will explain questions more fully, he may give you an example of an answer to a question, or he will simply become more relaxed when he poses questions and evaluates your answers. And if he's relaxed, it will be easier for you to act naturally as well!

Your personality can never take the place of being qualified for a position. However, if you have gotten this far—if you've been asked in for an interview—then you probably have some skills the employer already finds desirable. She will be interviewing other people who have similar skills as you do. Your personality can push you to the top of her list, even if you aren't the *most* qualified person. The family metaphor is useful, again, when thinking about this. If your family supported themselves by farming, would you want to invite an excellent farmer with an unsavory personality into your family? Or would you want to invite an adequate famer who would be willing to work hard and at the same time be someone you would enjoy spending time with?

As your résumé, you should do your best to target your personality to the job position that you are applying for. This means you may want to highlight different aspects of your personality, depending on the job. A salesperson, for example, has to be very outgoing and sociable. For a software engineer, this does not matter as much. This doesn't mean you pretend to be someone you're not, though. If your natural personality is not really suitable for the job, then you should probably not be applying for the job in the first place!

Interview
→

Even if you're nervous, be friendly and polite. When people find you likeable, they're also more likely to offer you the job.

While some personality traits may be more appropriate for some job settings more than others, almost all employers value certain qualities. These include confidence, **approachability**, a sense of humor, trustworthiness, and leadership. As you discuss

Looking at the Words

Approachability is how easy you are to talk to and do business with.

your past experiences and relevant knowledge, make sure to keep these qualities in mind—and mind your manners! Demonstrating your sense of humor in a job interview, for example, is not about cracking jokes of your own but about laughing if your interviewer makes a humorous comment (even if it is not very funny).

There is no definite formula for interview success. Just be as relaxed, friendly, and respectful as possible.

CHAPTER 5

Looking to the Future

When you're looking for a job, the future can seem like a terribly scary time. For some people (depending on their field of work), looking for a job can become a job in and of itself. It can be stressful to have to spend your time this way.

Stress is one of the main reasons that people act out angrily or violently. It is also one of the main reasons people forget to use their manners and etiquette. If you are becoming stressed, there are things you can do: talk to a friend, take a walk, exercise, meditate, or pray. If necessary, see a

doctor or a counselor. When you're relaxed, you will see your manners and etiquette greatly improve. You can be your best self!

The future may seem confusing and frightening sometimes—but the future is also full of new opportunities. Do your best to take advantage of them.

The Future of Communications

The technology that we are using to communicate is advancing rapidly, more rapidly perhaps than our manners and etiquette. From the cell phone to your e-mail to social networking sites, all of these have the possibility of factoring into your employment situation.

Most young people today have spent most of their lives using technologies like this. This can be a benefit because young people can use these technologies with a lot more confidence than older applicants. Skills with these technologies can even be listed on a résumé because they are becoming more and more useful, for many reasons, for a great number of fields. On the other hand, unsavory information about you (even if it is long in your past) can be kept on websites like this. Make sure that any representation of yourself on a social networking website is something that you wouldn't mind showing your boss!

Compared to technologies that have been around longer—the phone for example—no rules of etiquette are considered universal for technologies like social networking websites. But this is all the more reason to make sure that your manners are top-notch. Proper manners, no matter what medium they are being communicated in, will always be noticed. In a world where manners seem to matter less and less, they only be-

come all the more useful. Good manners can make you stand out from the crowd.

Following Up

Following up after an interview is a great way to ensure that you're remembered. Write and mail a thank-you note to anyone who has interviewed you. Even if you're not chosen for the position, you want to make sure that the company remembers you as positively as possible. If they have job openings in the future, they may remember you and give you a call.

Interviewing skills, like all skills, need to be practiced. Maybe you were so nervous at your last interview that you froze and couldn't think of any answers to the questions posed to you. Don't let it get you down. Think of it as a learning experience. Next time, you'll know more what to expect, and you won't be as nervous.

If someone you know helped you get the interview, make sure you thank him or her for helping you, even if you didn't get the job. Building a strong network is one of the best ways to protect your future. The more people who know you and like you, the more job opportunities will be likely to come your way.

And how do you get more people to like you? By presenting yourself as best you can—with good manners, good etiquette, and respect—in each and every situation you find yourself. You never know what could lead to a job!

Find Out More

In Books

Bjorkman, Steve, Peggy Post and Cindy Post Senning. *Emily Post's Guide to Good Manners for Kids*. New York: HarperCollins Publishers, 2004.

Sonneborn, Liz. *Nonverbal Communication: The Art of Body Language (Communicating With Confidence)*. New York: Rosen Publishing Group, 2011.

Travis, Dr. Richard L. *Tech Etiquette: OMG (Dr T's Living Well Series)*. New York: RLT Publishing, 2012.

On the Internet

Career Kids: Career Information
www.careerkids.com/careers

Easy Etiquette for Preteens: Minding Your Manners
www.pamf.org/preteen/growingup/etiquette.html

Kids.gov
kids.usa.gov/teens-home/index.html

Bibliography

Ellis, Blake. "Average Student Loan Debt Nears $27,000." *CNNMoney*, October 18, 2012. http://money.cnn.com/2012/10/18/pf/college/student-loan-debt/index.html (accessed April 1, 2013).

Kingkade, Tyler. "Mitt Romney's Debate Claim on College Grad Unemployment Was Almost Accurate." *The Huffington Post*. October 17, 2012. http://www.huffingtonpost.com/2012/10/17/mitt-romney-college-graduate-unemployment-jobs_n_1973765.html (accessed April 2, 2013).

Mitchell, Nancy R. "Top 10 Interview Tips from an Etiquette Professional." *Experience*. http://www.experience.com/entry-level-jobs/jobs-and-careers/interview-resources/top-10-interview-tips-from-an-etiquette-professional/ (accessed April 3, 2013).

Tamny, John. "Sorry Left AND Right, No Job Requires a College Degree." *Forbes*, February 10, 2013. http://www.forbes.com/sites/johntamny/2013/02/10/sorry-left-and-right-no-job-requires-a-college-degree/ (accessed April 2, 2013).

U.S. Bureau of Labor Statistics. "College Enrollment and Work Activity of 2011 High School Graduates." http://www.bls.gov/news.release/hsgec.nr0.htm (accessed April 4, 2013).

wiseGeek.com. "What Should I Know About Business Etiquette?" http://www.wisegeek.com/what-should-i-know-about-business-etiquette.htm (accessed April 3, 2013).

wiseGeek.com. "What Should I Know About Business Etiquette in China?" http://www.wisegeek.com/what-should-i-know-about-business-etiquette-in-china.htm (accessed April 3, 2013).

Index

About the Author

Christie Marlowe lives in Binghamton, New York, where she works as a writer and web designer. She has a degree in literature, cares strongly about the environment, and spends three or more nights a week wailing on her Telecaster.

Picture Credits